The Four W...

NORTH INCH AND THE LANDS OF THE BLACKFRIARS

THE CITY CENTRE

THE SOUTH INCH TO THE A.K. BELL LIBRARY

TAY STREET AND THE BRIDGES

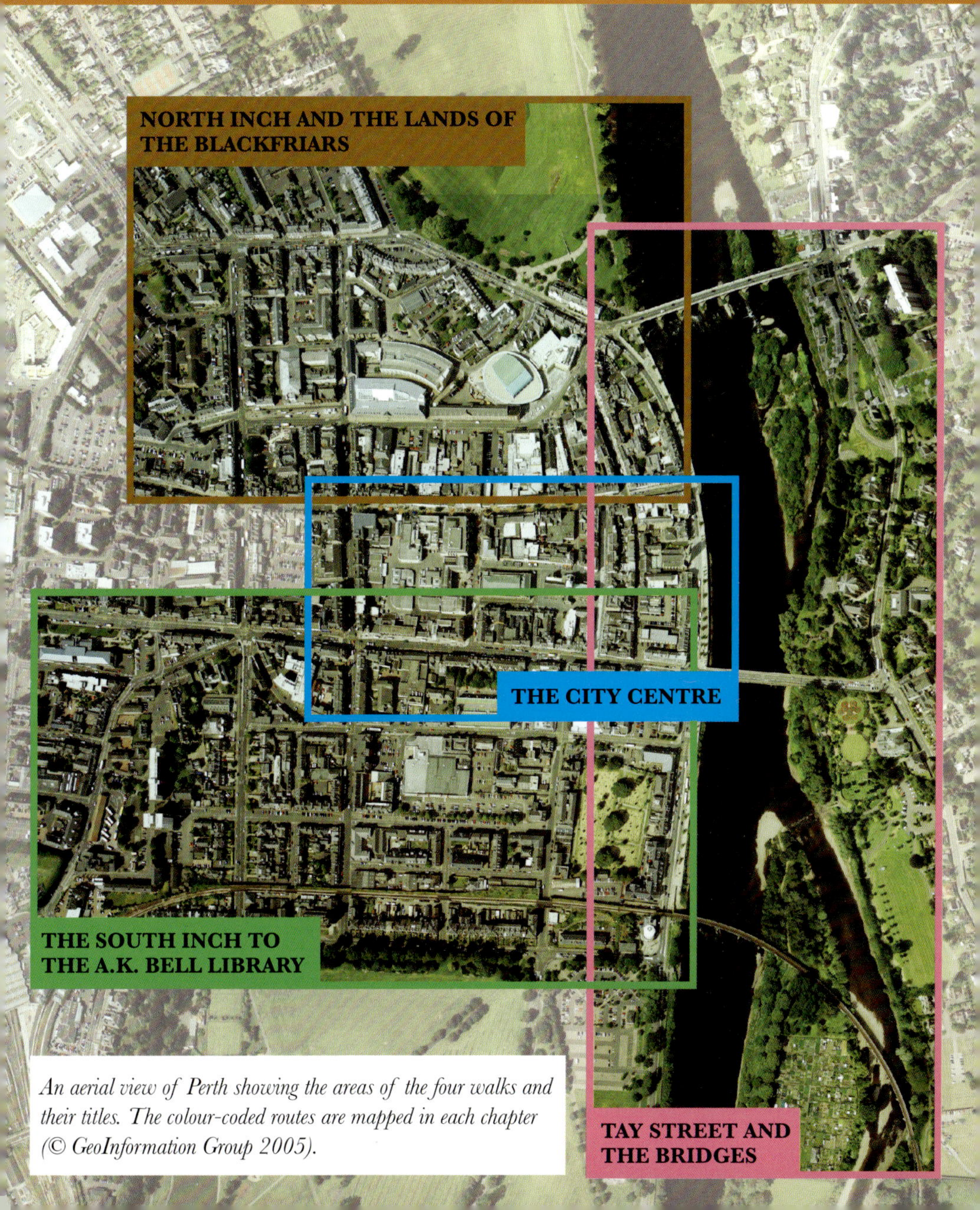

An aerial view of Perth showing the areas of the four walks and their titles. The colour-coded routes are mapped in each chapter (© GeoInformation Group 2005).

The City Centre

This walk leads you through the older parts of Perth lying within the Royal Burgh. It begins at the west door of **St. John's Kirk (1)**, the historic Burgh Kirk of Perth. The earliest record for the Kirk is 1128 when it was gifted by David I of Scotland to the Benedictine monks of Dunfermline Abbey who then had the right to appoint a rector, and the duty to care for the fabric of the church. Being within the diocese of St. Andrews there is a record of re-consecration by Bishop de Bernham in 1242.

After the struggle for Scottish Independence King Robert the Bruce, in 1328, ordered the repair of the church requesting stone from Kincarrathie Quarry near Scone.

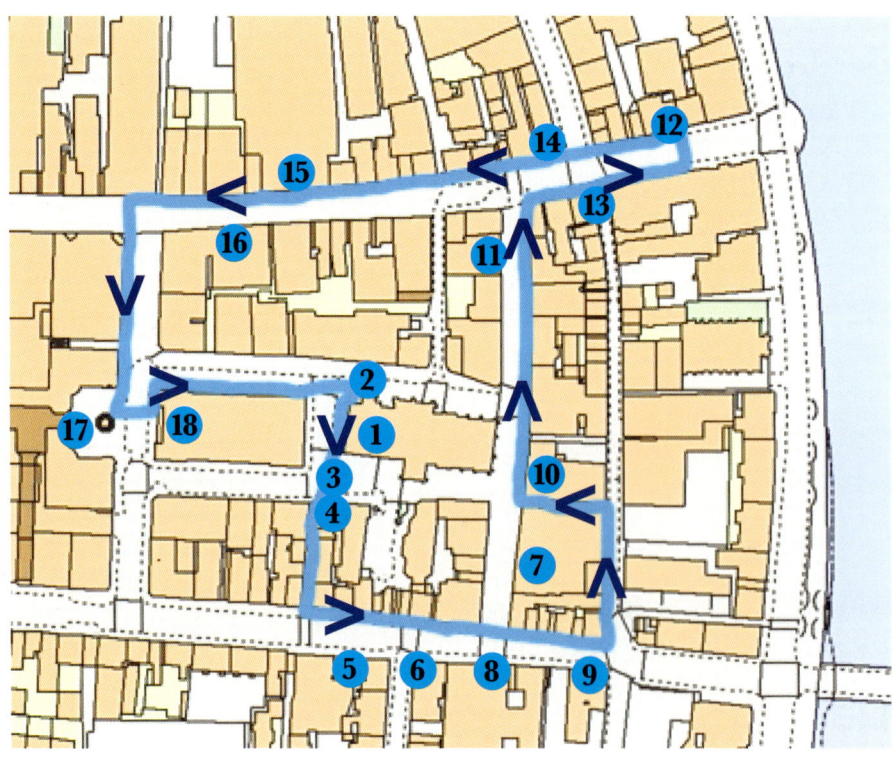

The City Centre walk of around 1.2km, showing buildings of interest numbered in the text (© Crown copyright and database right 2009. All rights reserved. 100016971).

① © *PKHT*

Early Royal Charters, by granting rights, increased the trade and prosperity of Perth which encouraged burgesses and merchant traders to commence reconstruction of the earlier church. What stands here today reflects that major undertaking. The choir at the east end, the ceremonial part of the church, contains the high altar and was complete by 1448. The crossing and the square tower with its splay-footed broach spire were finished by 1511. The west part, the nave, followed thereafter. The interior of that medieval church had richly painted plastered walls and richly carved furnishings – altars, screens and pews for the clergy.

Reproduced courtesy of A.K. Bell Local Studies Dept.

Ideas for a new Reformed Church spread from Europe

and St. John's Kirk played an important part in the Reformation when John Knox delivered his sermon against idolatry from there on 11th May 1559. Standing immediately outwith the walls of the town were the pre-Reformation religious Houses of the Grey and Black Friars and the Carthusian monks. All were attacked by riotous and frenzied crowds roused by Knox's sermon. Inside the Kirk today remain relics of that pre-Reformation Church – a stone niche, holy water stoups and piscinas, consecration crosses and masons' marks.

Seating for the congregation in the Reformed Church was provided, and by the end of the 16th century repairs to the church nave included a partition to form the West Church. By 1604 the patronage and income of the church had been gifted to the Provost and Magistrates of Perth by Queen Ann, wife of James VI of Scotland and I of England.

Royalty attended services in St. John's Kirk: Charles I and Charles II in the 17th century, and Charles Edward Stuart in 1745 during his brief stay in Perth at the period of the Jacobite Rising. By the end of the 18th century the Kirk contained three separate churches: West, Middle and East. Towards the end of Victorian times there was a growing desire to remove the two partition walls and restore the original form of one church, however, this was not achieved until after the First World War.

In 1926 the Scottish architect Sir Robert Lorimer completed the planned restoration of St. John's Kirk, which was Perth's War Memorial, and incorporated the Memorial Shrine with the Golden Book listing the names of the Fallen. At the east end of the church, following the Second World War, the Knox Chapel was dedicated to those who had died in that conflict.

If you have time and the Kirk is open it is well worth a visit.

Looking at the west door walk to the left of the Kirk and look at **Halkerston's Tower (2)**, part of the restoration work and designed by Sir Robert Lorimer to mark the position of a late 15th century tower

 © PKHT

3 © *PKHT*

probably built by Halkerston, the King's Master Mason. Look up to the church tower where a bartizan belfry houses a collection of silent bells dating from the 14th century onwards. In 1935 a fine new carillon of 34 bells was installed in the Kirk Tower with the Bourdon Bell dated 1506 and inscribed, in Latin, "made in Mechlin by Peter de Waghevens". Inscribed on the leaded spire above the belfry are the names of 18th century members of the Town Council.

Pre-Reformation, the area in front of the church was the town's burial ground, and any excavation here usually uncovers human bone. By 1580 the abandoned site of the House of the Greyfriars, just outside the south wall of the town, had been acquired as Perth's new burial ground. The site of the old burial ground later became the Fleshmarket with Fleshers' Vennel leading to South Street. On the left corner of Fleshers' Vennel, the fine red sandstone building with Dutch gable, built in 1910, was the **Kirk Session House of St. John's (3)**. Further left is the

4 © *PKHT*

distinctive modern office building on three floors occupied in 1978 by the General Accident Fire and Life Assurance Company and now offices of the Perthshire Housing Association. The reflection of historic St. John's Kirk can be seen in the tall smoked-glass windows. St. Ann's Lane, by the side of this building, was the site of the pre-Reformation Chapel of St. Ann.

The walk continues into Fleshers' Vennel leading to South Street. Almost immediately you will see to your left above a shop window the thistle medallion from **Perth's Mercat Cross (4)**, which was dismantled in 1765. The medallion was then used as a marriage lintel and dated 1766. As you reach South Street note the symbolism of the ox-head on the bollard at South Street and glance across to the red sandstone tenement where a panel displaying the tools of the **Flesher Incorporation (5)** is seen above the first floor window. To the right of this Cow Vennel links the route from the cattle grazing on the South Inch to Fleshers' Vennel and the Fleshmarket established in 1761.

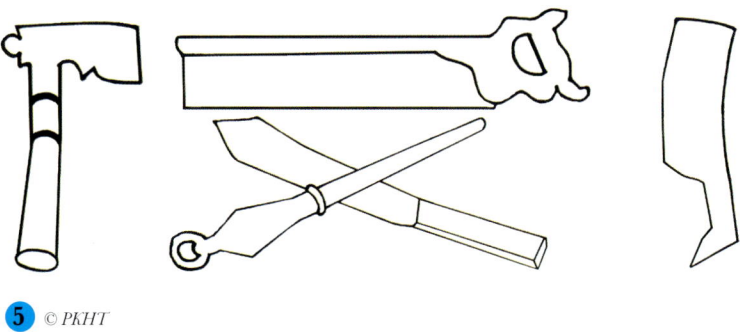

5 © *PKHT*

Turn left into South Street and walk towards Princes Street along which, in the 1760s, came the new approach from Edinburgh via Friarton and the South Inch. On the corner of South Street and Princes Street is the former **Commercial Bank of Scotland (6)** designed by David Rhind. Interesting features are the bearded heads at the keystones of the window arches of the ground floor. Facing Princes Street the large three storey building was strategically placed as the City Hotel in the early 19th century, ready to accommodate visitors arriving by stagecoach or river steamer.

7 © *Courtesy of McEwens of Perth*

You now reach St. John Street, formed at the end of the 18th century and linking South Street to George Street and Smeaton's Bridge. This was a spacious improvement on the old route via the narrow medieval Watergate. Opposite you is **McEwens of Perth (7)**. Look up to the inscription in a first floor window which marks the site of the 15th century Town House and garden (with fountain) of the Bishops of Dunkeld. The old house was demolished in 1821 but the entrance to it from South Street remains as Fountain Close. The corner shop frontage of 1906 is in ornate style and the window frames are worthy of note. This is an early 19th century tenement with an interesting chimney gable facing the street.

Pausing here look across South Street to the interesting frontage of **The Salutation Hotel (8)** facing St. John Street. The earlier inn had links to the Jacobite Rising of 1745, the two figures - an officer and a piper of the Black Watch – being reminders of that event. They formed part of an enlarged façade of the early 19th century which included the splendid window with fanlight above and a stone balustrade at the roof.

To the left of the Salutation Hotel are mid-18th century tenements – the first with a chimney gable similar to those in St. John Street. Beyond the gap site is a double tenement with crow-stepped gable. Of the two ground floor shops note the **bow-windowed shop front (9)** the only one remaining in Perth and one of very few in Scotland.

Continue along South Street to Watergate on your left and Speygate on your right. These two streets formed the medieval route from Canal Street to High Street. Turn into Watergate which lies parallel to the Tay and where the waterfront was of commercial importance in medieval times. Here were the homes of craftsmen, merchants and professionals as well as the town houses of local lairds and landowners. The gardens of houses on the right extended to the riverside and by 1872 had become part of the embankment for Tay Street.

Narrow passageways led to the river, as the Water Vennel still does, giving a glimpse of Tay Street. On the corner of the Water Vennel there stood, until 1965, the 17th century Town House of George Hay, 1st Earl of Kinnoull, a stone building of three storeys with projecting wooden frontage at the two upper floors. Turn left into Baxter's Vennel where the Baxter Incorporation had their Meeting Hall. You now reach St. John Street again where, on your right, the prestigious former **Central Bank of Scotland (10)** (1846-47), designed by David Rhind and sympathetically converted by Lakeland, dominates the street. Stand back to view the fine palazzo architecture – the stone balustrades and balcony, the Corinthian pilasters and elaborate pediments making an impressive statement. On the other side of the Bank lies Oliphant's Vennel referring to a Perthshire family with staunch Jacobite sympathies.

10 © PKHT

 © PKHT

Most of the buildings on St. John Street are late Georgian and although shop fronts have been restored or renewed, the street, in a conservation area, retains its former period look when genteel shops provided fashionable and desirable goods for ladies and gentlemen. Walk towards the High Street and on your left there is a fine building, originally the **Bank of Scotland (11)**, with ornate cast iron balcony and columned entrances. The left hand door has its original fanlight.

At the High Street turn right and walk towards the river. At the foot of the High Street were the quays of the North Shore where trading began before the 12th century. The 1124 Charter of David I created a Royal Burgh and granted privileges which increased trade. Exports of hides, leather, wool and salmon and imports of corn, wine, timber and iron made Perth one of the richest early Royal Burghs, its revenue yield coming mainly from ship customs. Permission to hold markets and fairs was also given.

The Merchant Guild - now The Guildry Incorporation of Perth – formed by Royal Charter was entrusted with the administration and regulation of the town and developed into Perth Town Council.

The Royal Bank of Scotland (12), on your left near the foot of the High Street, stands on the former site of the Town House of the Stormont family of Scone, where Prince Charles Edward Stuart lodged briefly in September 1745 before proceeding south with his army in the Jacobite Rising. Outside the bank, in the middle of the street, a circular 'Perth Pillory' stone can be seen sunk into the road surface, a reminder of medieval punishment meted out at the foot of the High Street.

Return to the corner of Watergate and look up at the building which marks the site of the **Town House of the Mercer family (13)**, merchant traders recorded as gifting in the 11th century their corn and flour mills in Perth to King Malcolm III. Their armorial bearings are above the central first floor window. The frontage was

re-styled in the 19th century. Look across the High Street to the corner building on High Street and George Street with a gable dated 1774 **(14)**. From here to Skinnergate are five tenements, all late 18th century of varying styles. These are what surely prompted a traveller in 1792 to describe the High Street as "striking and of grand effect where lived the merchants and manufacturers".

Skinnergate and Kirkgate, on the other side of the High Street, formed the route in early times from the castle, destroyed by flood in 1210, to the Kirk of St. John. A cross, sunk into the middle of the street, marks the site of Perth's Mercat Cross which was demolished by Cromwell for use in building his Citadel on the South Inch in 1651. This was replaced by a new cross in 1665 only to be demolished again in 1765.

On market days the street was thronged with people and packed with stalls, all closely controlled by the Merchant Guild's defining rules. Quality was inspected by ale tasters and meal searchers and quantity by overseers of weights and measures. If found to be breaking the laws traders paid fines, had goods confiscated or even their stalls destroyed. By 1761 the Fleshmarket had relocated, as had the Butter and Cheese Market, and permanent shops replaced mobile traders.

15 © R. Fothergill

In 1975-79 an excavation was carried out before the new Marks & Spencer store was opened in 1981. A 16th century stone-built merchant's house referred to as 'Parliament Hall' had stood on this site **(15)**. Archaeologists soon uncovered its foundations and, further below, the remains of 12th century timber buildings.

Opposite Marks and Spencer is an interesting streetscape of four, four-storey-high tenements. Each has an architecturally different and distinctive frontage. Further along a restored frontage of a late 18th century tenement, by contrast, is lower and has smaller windows. Standing next to this is the grand frontage of the **Guild Hall of 1906 (16)**. It replaced the first Guild Hall of 1722 in a good position, at that time, to overlook the market stalls of the High Street, the trading centre of Perth.

1990 saw the pedestrianisation of the High Street and a new look of planted trees, seats and sculptures. At the end of the Skinnergate, seated on a bench, is 'The Fair Maid of Perth', a bronze figure of Catharine Glover, daughter of Simon Glover, Deacon of the Glover Incorporation – both fictitious characters in Sir Walter Scott's novel of that name. Opposite King Edward Street is a sculpture inspired by the Perth poet William Soutar and his poem 'Nae Day Sae Dark'.

16 © PKHT

Late 19th century Town Improvement Acts brought about the clearance of an area of narrow closes and poor, overcrowded housing and by 1901 King Edward Street, named with royal consent, was formed. Looking along King Edward Street the modern department store on the right hand corner was erected after extensive excavation work to 12th century levels.

17 © PKHT

Walk along King Edward Street until you reach the open space on your right where you will see **Perth's Mercat Cross (17)** which was re-instated in 1913 and incorporates the memorial to King Edward VII. The Cross bears the insignia and mottoes of Perth Incorporations and has a tall shaft surmounted by a unicorn holding a shield. Behind is an entrance to St. John's Shopping Mall, opened in 1988.

18 *Reproduced courtesy of A.K. Bell Local Studies Dept.*

Opposite this, and dominating King Edward Street, is **Perth City Hall (18)**, built on the site of an earlier City Hall and the old Fleshmarket. It is a substantial building erected to the plans of H.E. Clifford, a Glasgow architect. Behind a frontage of impressive columns are three entrance doors. Opened in 1911 it contained a main hall with a smaller hall to the rear.

Sadly, following the opening of the Concert Hall in 2005, the building is no longer used and is currently the subject of various redevelopment and demolition proposals.

To the left, the building on the corner was erected in 1933, over 20 years after the opening of the City Hall, during which time the site was unleased owing to the recession which followed the First World War. The architect's design has plain columns at the upper floors and complemented the City Hall.

Return along North St. John's Place, now a café quarter for visitors and residents, to St. John's Kirk, one of Perth's finest assets, the history of which links to and reflects the historical, political and social events in the lives of the people of Perth.

North Inch and the Lands of the Blackfriars

Until the end of the 18th century Perth was contained within its medieval boundaries of Canal Street, Methven Street, Mill Street and the River Tay. There were activities outside the area such as weavers' houses in New Row, mills on the site of the City Mills Hotel and the grounds that had belonged to the Blackfriars near the North Inch, but they were all in these positions for a particular reason.

At the end of the 18th century there was a rise in population all over Scotland and new housing was needed. Edinburgh had started to build its 'New Town' and so had Perth, albeit on a more modest scale. Despite the lack of grandeur Perth's Georgian buildings are said to be some of the finest outside Edinburgh. The architecture was the currently fashionable 'Georgian' style based on classical models made famous by the Adam brothers. Houses had 'mod cons' such as inside stairs and water closets.

This walk starts at the dry arch of **Smeaton's Bridge (19)**. Until Tay Street was built and the river bank was raised the River Tay was much wider and there was frequent flooding each winter with the marks on the wall of the dry arch of the bridge noting some of the more recent heights.

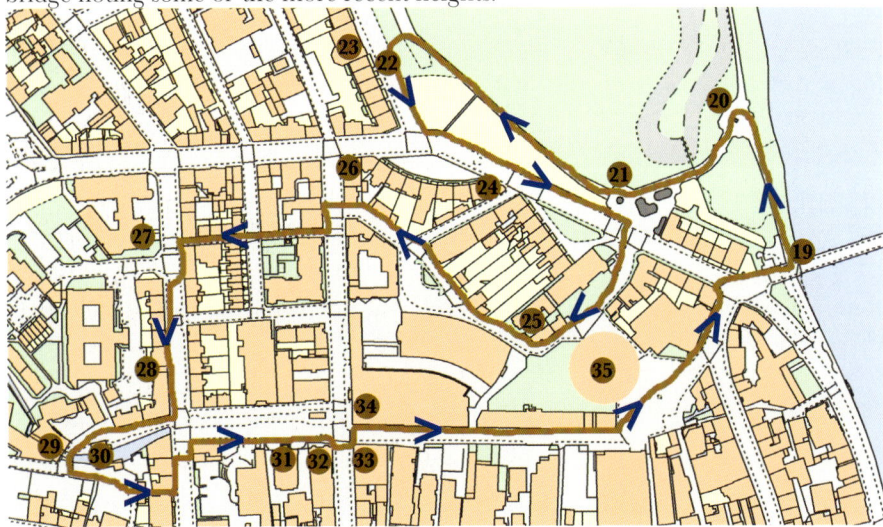

The North Inch and Blackfriars walk of around 2.1km, showing buildings of interest numbered in the text (© Crown copyright and database right 2009. All rights reserved. 100016971).

Walk along the path towards the North Inch. The word inch comes from the Gaelic term for island and means a piece of land by a river. This was originally a far smaller area but reached its present size in 1803 as a result of an excambion, or exchange of lands, with the Earl of Kinnoull. The Inch has been frequently flooded but this has not happened since the extensive works following the major flooding of 1993. You will notice the raised bank on the river side of the Inch and the flood gates – all part of these works.

Almost immediately you come to the **Lynedoch Monument (20)** on your left. This is Egyptian in style with an obelisk, and was unveiled in 1896 in memory of the 90th Perthshire Light Infantry. The Infantry, which later became the 2nd Battalion of the Cameronians, was raised by Thomas Graham who later became the 1st Lord Lynedoch. Further to the left is the memorial to the 51st Highland Division which has long standing links with the area. This Memorial is a replica of a statue unveiled in Holland showing a Dutch girl offering flowers to a Scottish soldier carrying his bagpipes, and is in memory of the Division's contribution during the Second World War. The Memorial also notes the contribution of the 51st Highland Division to the defeat of the Afrika Corps at El Alamein.

Walk through the flood gates towards Atholl Street and you will see the statue of **Prince Albert (21)**, unveiled by Queen Victoria in 1864. The Prince is shown wearing the robes of the Order of the Thistle and holding the plans of the Crystal Palace Exhibition. This section of the path used to be called Horse Watering Road as it was the route by which horses were taken to the river to drink. Next to Prince Albert is a large modern sculpture of thistles – a piece of work commissioned by Perthshire Public Arts Trust.

21 © PKHT

17

22 © *PKHT*

Turn to your right and walk along the path with the Inch on the right. This leads to **Rose Terrace (22)**, a Georgian terrace completed in 1807. The central part of this housed the original **Perth Academy (23)** and in 1886 the Britannia sculpture was installed on the top. In front of the Academy is another piece of public art work with stones, engraved with poems, being set into the shape of a circle. You could, if you wish, walk further along the path towards Bell's Sports Centre and Balhousie Castle, now the Black Watch Museum. At the far end of the Inch is a golf course.

Walk to the left along the grass of the Inch towards Atholl Street. Across the road is Atholl Crescent, a fine crescent of Georgian houses. On the extreme left of the crescent is the home of the **Royal Perth Golfing Society (24)** – one of the oldest golf clubs in Scotland, having been established in 1824, and which, in 1833, was the first in the world to be granted royal status. The only indication that this is the Society's headquarters is the Society's crest etched on four of the ground floor windows.

23 © *PKHT*

At the end of Rose Terrace is a stone plinth with a plaque commemorating 'The Battle of the Clans' in 1396. It seems that a fight to the death was an accepted way of settling disputes which had not been amenable to any other solution. The opposing groups on this occasion were Clan Chattan and Clan Kay, with 30 men on each side. One of the Clan Chattan men deserted and Hal O' the Wynd took his place, as described by Sir Walter Scott in his novel The Fair Maid of Perth. Further along Atholl Street, to your left, is a second stone plinth with a plaque commemorating the uprisings of 1715 and 1745 when the Jacobites assembled on the Inch.

Cross the road to Blackfriars Street and note the plaque on the left hand corner giving a little information about the Blackfriars. This is all part of the area of the monastery grounds. Walk further along Atholl Street to Charlotte Place. Notice the interesting corner building with its curved structure, pillars and wrought ironwork on the first floor. Turn right here and walk into North Port, the original northern entry to the town. You will notice, on your left, the new Concert Hall, opened in 2005. On your right is Lord John Murray House, now the home of the Royal Scottish Geographical Society. Lord John Murray was one of Perth's members of Parliament in the mid-18th century. Adjoining this is **Fair Maid's House (25)**, made famous by Sir Walter Scott in his novel. The present house, the oldest secular building in the city, was built on the site of earlier buildings, and at least part of it dates back to 1475 and is mentioned in the records of the Blackfriars. The inscription above the door reads "Grace and Peace", the motto of the Glover Incorporation who owned the building and used it as a meeting hall.

 © PKHT

Carry on walking up to Blackfriars Wynd with the multi-storey parking on your left and on through Carpenter Street to Kinnoull Street. Cross over and look back to your left. The restaurant on the corner of Kinnoull Street and Atholl Street is the **site of the original Perth Theatre (26)** which opened in 1820. In 1828 *The Fair Maid of Perth* was performed there. Sadly the theatre was closed in 1844.

Walk up the lane beside you (Union Lane) to North Methven Street. Across the road is the Scottish Episcopal **Cathedral of St. Ninian (27)**. A London architect, William Butterfield, designed the building and, consecrated in 1850, it was the first post-Reformation cathedral constructed in Britain. The ground it stands on was originally part of Blackfriars. If you have time and the cathedral is open the stained glass windows are well worth looking at. There is also more detailed information available in the cathedral.

Cross the road, turn left and walk along North Methven Street to Mill Street. Just before you reach this you will notice a pend on your right **(28)** – this was used for access to the land behind the buildings which was occupied by Wright's Brewery from the late-18th century up until after the Second World War. Turn right into Mill Street, noticing the lade on the other side of the street, and you see the imposing buildings of the mills.

27 © PKHT

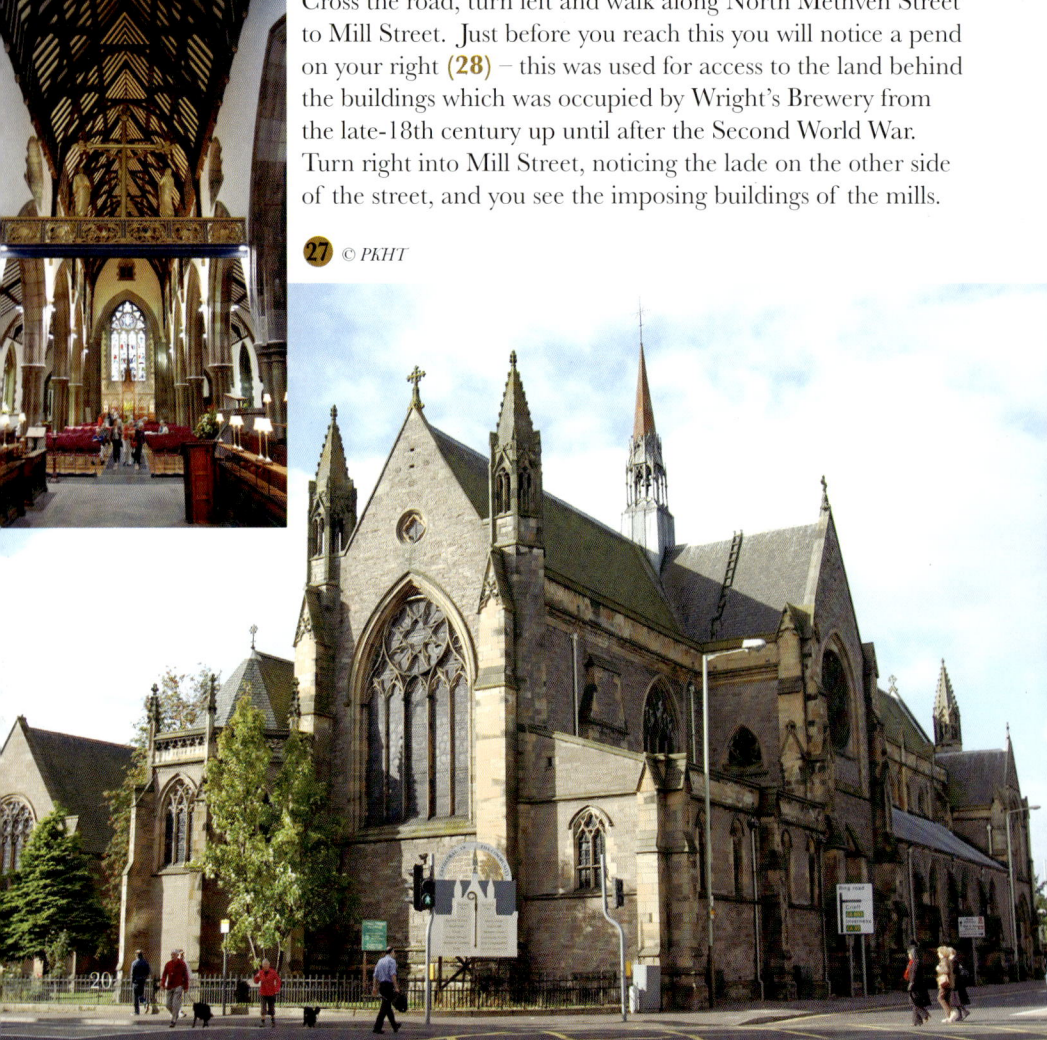

 © PKHT

The **Upper City Mills (29)** 1774-92 (now a hotel) comprised two flour mills and opposite this is a three-storey, five-bay granary with a projecting frontage to accommodate a hoist. In the hotel two undershot water wheels are visible below the foyer and a splendid king-post roof survives above the ballroom. It is certainly worth going in to have a look if you have time. The two **Lower City Mills (30)**, currently housing the Visitor Information Centre, were completed in 1805 and used for milling oatmeal and pot barley. By the Second World War the main production was animal feed. You can still see the large water wheel and until the flood prevention works at the beginning of this century the Mill was still used – mainly as a visitor attraction.

Walk past the Upper City Mills and round the Lower Mills where you will see, over to your right, the steeple of St. Paul's Church, a most unusual octagonal church opened

 © PKHT

in 1807 but now sadly in need of major repair and restoration. In front of you is the gable end of Hal O' the Wynd's house, yet another fanciful linking to *The Fair Maid of Perth* – walk through the close here and back onto North Methven Street. Turn left and then right onto Murray Street. Walking down here you pass the **North Church (31)** on your right and then on the corner of Murray Street and Kinnoull Street is what used to be the **Sandeman Library (32)**, until it moved to new premises as the A.K. Bell Library, and is now a pub. The building opposite that, yet another pub and restaurant, used to house the headquarters of **Matthew Gloag & Son Ltd (33)**, creators of the Famous Grouse. On the other corner is the impressive façade of what used to be the **Pullars of Perth headquarters (34)**. This building was bought and converted in the 1990s and now houses offices of Perth and Kinross Council.

Cross Kinnoull Street and walk down Mill Street noticing that the Pullars façade carries on right down the street. At the end of this building you pass the main entrance of **Perth Concert Hall (35)**. This was once the site of the original Horsecross – Perth's 17th century horse market. The name has been retained by the umbrella organisation which runs the Concert Hall and the Theatre. To the right is the Red Brig where the Lade surfaces briefly again before flowing into the Tay. Walk up to George Street and cross it, noticing on your left Perth Art Gallery and Museum (explanation in the "Tay Street Walk") and continue to Tay Street and Smeaton's Bridge where your walk started.

22

34 © *PKHT*

35 © *PKHT*

23

The South Inch to the A.K. Bell Library

We start this walk at the corner of Marshall Place and Tay Street with the South Inch on one side and **The Fergusson Gallery (36)**, or Round House, on the other. The South Inch was outside the southern boundary of the medieval burgh of Perth, within which there were strict rules governing trading and industrial activity. Outside the boundary other communities and activities developed and the South Inch was a busy place where these were many and varied. Cattle were grazed, cloth was laid out for bleaching and, until the late-18th century, when it was moved to the North Inch, there was horse-racing. Archery competitions were held, in 1842 Perth Curling Club developed a pond for winter curling and, until about 1850, golf was also played here. We do not know how all these activities were kept apart and the area was regularly flooded. Both the North and South Inches had been granted to Perth by charter from Robert III in 1377. In the early 1650s Oliver Cromwell was proclaimed Lord Protector and an enormous fort was built at the South Inch to defend the river approach to Perth. It covered a vast area adjacent to the river and part of this was excavated prior to the flood defence works. Sadly there is no visible evidence of this remaining today.

The South Inch to A.K. Bell Library walk of around 1.1km, showing buildings of interest numbered in the text (© Crown copyright and database right 2009. All rights reserved. 100016971).

37 © PKHT

The Fergusson Gallery was originally the waterworks for Perth. It was designed in the style of a Roman Doric Temple by Adam Anderson, Rector of Perth Academy, in the early-19th century. Water was filtered in beds on Moncreiffe Island in the River Tay and then it was pumped by steam engines into the large cast iron tank at the top of the building and then fed by gravity to water pumps. A supply of water to the town started in 1832. Above the door is an inscription "Aquam igne et aqua haurio" (By fire and water I draw water). Note the interesting urn on top of the chimney. The building became redundant in 1965 when the water works were moved and, following an outcry over threatened demolition, major renovation work was undertaken and the building became the Tourist Office. Following the relocation of the Tourist Office it became The Fergusson Gallery, providing a home for the main collection of paintings by J.D. Fergusson (1874-1961), the Scottish colourist, and gifted to Perth and Kinross Council by the Trustees of the J.D. Fergusson Art Foundation. Outside the Gallery is an enlarged copy of the sculpture "Torse de Femme" by Fergusson (1918).

Walk away from the river until you reach Princes Street which, along with Edinburgh Road, formed the main entrance into the City from the south. In 1842 Queen Victoria and Prince Albert visited Perth and a Triumphal Arch, made of painted wood and canvas, was constructed at this end of Princes Street. The keys to the city were presented to the Queen and Prince Albert was given the freedom of Perth.

Thomas Hay Marshall was one of the enterprising men who financed the building of new highly desirable houses in the town, and these can be seen in **Marshall Place (37)**. They were designed by Robert Reid and were built in two symmetrical blocks, houses (1-14) and (15-28). They were built of stone with lunette attic windows, tall chimney stacks and astragals along the roof edge. In Marshall Mews, behind the houses, were stable blocks, and the original cobblestones are still visible **(38)**.

As you cross Scott Street, Marshall Place becomes King James Place and the fine style of houses continues. The church is **St Leonard's-in-the-Fields and Trinity (39)** erected in 1886 as St. Leonard's Free Church and later combining with Trinity Church. Note the superb crown steeple surmounting the square tower.

39 © PKHT

40 © PKHT

At the end of the road is the railway station. By 1845 the strategic importance of Perth to the various railway companies was being recognised. The Town Council wanted to encourage this method of transport and gain benefits for Perth. The South Inch was suggested as an ideal place for a station, but many citizens of Perth were not pleased about this and drew up a petition. By 1846 the railway companies realised that the site on the Inch had several disadvantages, such as regular flooding and the difference in levels from the Dundee line. The present site, situated on higher ground, was considered to be preferable. There also used to be a smaller station at Princes Street. The viaduct along which the railway runs can be seen at several points behind the houses facing the Inch.

Before you turn right into King Street, glance across the road where you will see a statue of Sir Walter Scott on the South Inch. Fine Georgian properties dated between 1830 and 1850 were built on King Street. As you near the end of King Street you will note, on your left, the former **St. Leonard's Parish Church (40)** (now occupied by Lindsey Burns Auctioneer) built in the Greek style with a choragic emblem on the top, and acting as a focal point at the end of Canal Street.

Before you turn left into Hospital Street (the former old road to Edinburgh until the early 1760s when the road was rerouted through the South Inch and Princes Street) notice, on the opposite side of the road Canal Crescent, one of the few curved streets in Perth, which marks the line of the lade taking water to the Tay. On Hospital Street is **King James VI Hospital (41)**, built on the site of the Charterhouse, a Carthusian Monastery, which was an enclosed silent order, founded by James I, and the only one in Scotland. The original foundation was at Chartreuse in France. The Carthusian Monastery site extended from King Street to Scott Street and Hospital Street to the South Inch. James I (1406-37) was murdered at Blackfriars Monastery and was buried in the grounds of the

41 © PKHT

29

Charterhouse, as was his wife, Joanne Beaufort. After the Reformation the lands of the Monastery ceased to function and King James VI founded a hospital. This was never a hospital in the modern sense but a charitable institution providing food and shelter. Its income was derived from rental on properties and land in and around Perth which had previously belonged to the religious orders. The present building was erected in 1750, refurbished in 1974 and now contains 21 flats.

As you continue along Hospital Street turn right into the New Row. This was an area outside the burgh where the weaving industry was established using looms in thatched cottages. In 1758 the New Row Linen Manufacturing Company was established producing "fine sheeting".

The large building up on your left is now the **A.K. Bell Library (42)** but was built as the Perth City and County Infirmary in 1836 by city architect William MacKenzie. The building has a fine classical facade in polished ashlar, extending over two storeys and eleven bays. When Perth Royal Infirmary opened in 1914 the building was used as a military hospital during the First World War and then became the headquarters for Perth County Council. In the mid 1990s, following considerable restoration and extension work, it opened as the A.K. Bell Library. The library gets its name from Arthur K. Bell, of the whisky dynasty, who founded The Gannochy Trust which supported the reconstruction of the building, and is a major benefactor in the Perth area. The iron railings at the front of the library were only reinstated in 2009, nearly seventy years after their removal early in the Second World War to be melted down and used to make planes and ammunition.

The modest lodge-house **(43)** to the northeast, part of the original construction, was moved and rebuilt in its present position in 1867, and then in 2000 was converted to form offices for Perth & Kinross Heritage Trust.

Tay Street and the Bridges

We are not absolutely certain when Perth was founded but we know it was a flourishing burgh by the 12th century, and that it was granted a Royal Burgh Charter by King William the Lion of Scotland in 1210. It was founded where the river was shallow enough to be crossed readily but also at the furthest point affected by the tide so boats could navigate upstream from the sea. It was a walled town – partly for defence and partly to manage drainage – on three sides with the River Tay on the fourth side. The importance of a bridge at Perth is fairly obvious but with the Tay having the greatest average daily flow of any UK river (equivalent to the Clyde, Severn and Thames combined) these were often washed away when the river was in spate. There was a spell of about 150 years when there was no bridge at all and ferries were essential. There are now three bridges – Smeaton's Bridge completed in 1771, the Railway Bridge dating from 1862 and the Queen's Bridge inaugurated by our present Queen in 1960.

Tay Street, as we know it, was not completed until the 1870s and before this many houses in Watergate had gardens which sloped right down to the river, often with their own jetty or quay.

In 1993 there was major flooding in Perth and this brought about a complete revamp of Tay Street and the North Inch. This walk will take you right along Tay Street with the river on your left and buildings, both old and new, on your right. We start at the Perth end of **Smeaton's Bridge (44)** and if you want to check

44 © PKHT

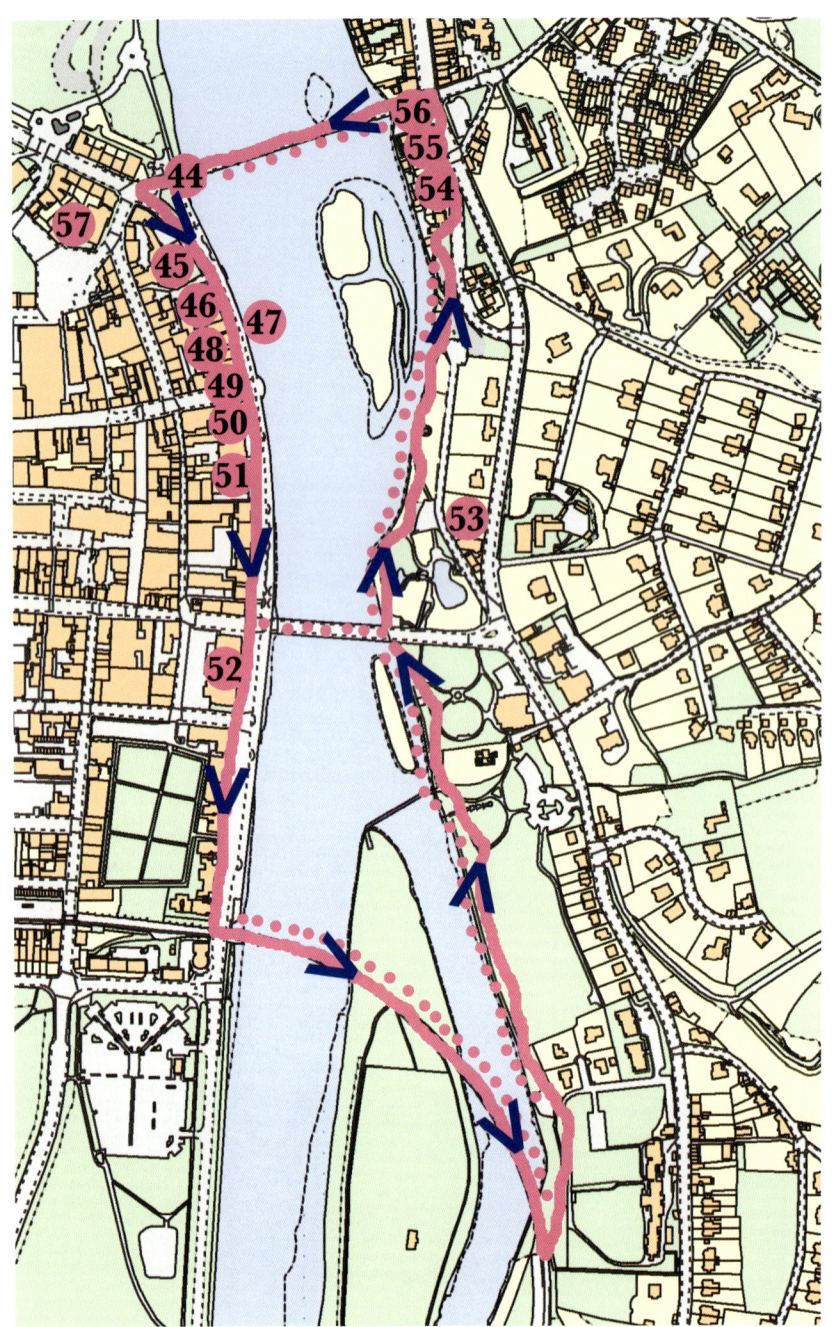

The Tay Street and the Bridges walk of around 2.7km, showing buildings of interest numbered in the text (© Crown copyright and database right 2009. All rights reserved. 100016971).

32

how high the various floods reached over the years walk down under the bridge and have a look at the marks on the bridge indicating the height the water reached and the year. Returning back up to Tay Street the first building of note we pass is the **Royal George Hotel (45)**. This had previously been called the George Inn but in 1848 bad weather upset royal travel plans and Queen Victoria and Prince Albert had to stop in Perth. The Queen agreed to stay at the George Inn and its name was subsequently changed. Next to the Royal George is the **Middle Church (46)**, converted to flats in 1995. It was built in 1886 as one of the second generation of free churches and the steeple is unique in Perth being shaped like a fleche or arrow.

46 © PKHT

The new wall along the river, part of the flood defences, runs from Smeaton's Bridge to Marshall Place at the South Inch, and there are fascinating carvings on the wall pillars based on references to various aspects of Perth life over the years. They are:

47 © *PKHT*

Pineapple (47) – David Douglas born in Scone in 1799 introduced many species of plants to Britain, including the Douglas Fir and Sikta Spruce. The pineapple relates to his tragic death, trampled by a bull in a pit in Hawaii. The pineapple was also thought to look like a pine cone, hence the name.

Unthank – Reference to a farm that existed within the city boundary.

Blue Kinnoull – Reference to the blue whinstone of Kinnoull and also Meconopsis grandis – the blue Himalayan poppy found in the National Trust for Scotland garden at Branklyn on the other side of the Tay off the Dundee Road.

Ecce Tiber – Reference to freshwater mussels and pearls, Perth being the pearl on the Tay. The Romans are alleged to have said Ecce Tiber when they first saw the Tay.

Gibralter – This depicts the bow of a boat representing the connection to Gibralter quay on the other side of the river. The bees signify the "Busy Bee" boat which ran up and down the Tay from Newburgh.

Cream of the Well – Represents water that was meant to hold special properties at a certain point of the year as noted in "Traditions of Perth" by George Penny in 1836.

Heart of Scotland – Perth's symbol as the heart of Scotland and the textures represent the contrast between the Highland and the Lowland physical landscape.

Tayberry – Represents the importance of the soft fruit industry to the area.

The Earth – One of Perth born poet William Soutar's best known poems.

Macnab – Reference to Perthshire's 'wildlife' – to catch a salmon, grouse and stag – all within a day is to be awarded the Macnab. This is taken from the novel "John Macnab" written by John Buchan who was born in Perth. The Mousetrap is the name of a pool further up the Tay renowned for its salmon.

The three sets of stainless steel gates to the fishing steps represent the wildlife and the landscapes associated with the Tay. There is also considerable planting of trees – mainly limes to replace those that were removed following the 1993 flooding.

There are a number of other pieces of artwork along Tay Street, many of which are explained on interpretation boards.

Just before you reach the promontory at the foot of the High Street look to the right and notice the stone archway leading into the pend where the town's fire-engines were based when they were still horsedrawn **(48)**.

The promontory opposite the Council Offices not only forms a focal point but is, perhaps, the centre piece of the redevelopment of Tay Street. Temporary flood gates are put into position at times of flood risk. The design of the railings has references to the town's maritime past, with this being the site of the earliest port in Perth. For centuries the town has had a port which, due to a build up of silt over the years, has gradually moved downstream to its present site at Friarton.

The two buildings on either side of the High Street are both Council buildings – the one on the right being known as the **Old Council Chambers (49)** has an interesting corner oriel and some magnificent stained glass windows. The building on the left is the new Council Chambers and was formerly the headquarters of **General Accident Fire and Life Assurance Corporation or G.A. (50)**.

Further along is **St. Matthew's Church (51)** built in 1871 and designed by John Honeyman. The undoubted glory of this church is its elegant 212ft tower and slender stone spire. As you approach the Queen's bridge notice another pend – this was the base of fish merchant Alexander Speedie who had easy access to the river from here with Water Vennel going right down to the river.

50 © PKHT

51 © PKHT

37

Crossing over South Street at the Queen's bridge you will be opposite the **Sheriff Court (52)**, or County Buildings, where many important trials have taken place. The architect of this building was Sir Robert Smirke (who also designed the British Museum) and both buildings are very much along Greek revival lines with magnificent pillars at the front. The trees here are Italian Alders mirroring the symmetry of these columns.

Many of the buildings along Tay Street, which were once offices of various kinds, have now been converted into flats. On the left hand side of Canal Street is Quayside Court, a sheltered housing development built on the site of a former Baptist Church destroyed by a spectacular fire in 1984. Prior to being bought by the Baptists the church had been an Opera House. This site had previously been part of the harbour known as the South (or Coal) Shore. Just along from there is the site of the first Museum of Natural History in Perth. This was opened by the Perthshire Society of Natural Science in 1883. In celebrating various anniversaries the Society was responsible for much of the tree planting on the north end of Moncreiffe Island which is directly opposite the building. At the junction of Canal Street and Tay Street was a quay where passenger ferries landed, and there is a branch of the Lade under Canal Street.

As you get towards the end of Tay Street you will see the railway bridge crossing the street and just before this, on your right, you will notice the impressive gateway into Greyfriars – a recently restored graveyard. If you have time climb up the steps to the bridge, cross over and do your return walk on the other side of the river. As you reach the top of the steps look over to the Fergusson Gallery on your right – a magnificent building about which you will find more information in the South Inch Walk.

The present railway bridge was opened in 1862/3 and prior to that, from 1849, there was a wooden bridge with a moveable span to accommodate shipping. Looking back along Tay Street from the bridge gives you a wonderful view of the city. Keep looking out too for seals and kingfishers both of which have been seen from the

bridge. Halfway along the bridge are steps down to Moncreiffe Island where there is a golf course – the King James VI Golf Club, so named because the King played "gowf" on the North Inch when the first course was laid out. The club moved to the island in 1897. Also on the island are a number of allotments. At the end of the bridge descend and turn left onto Riverside Walk. This leads you through Bellwood Riverside Park, gifted to the citizens of Perth by the GA. Rodney Lodge at its far end provided GA staff facilities when the Head Office was still in the High Street. There are various pieces of sculpture and artwork in the park and these were commissioned by the Perthshire Public Arts Trust.

You can at this point go up to the road and return to the centre of town via the Queen's Bridge, but if you have time carry on along the footpath under the

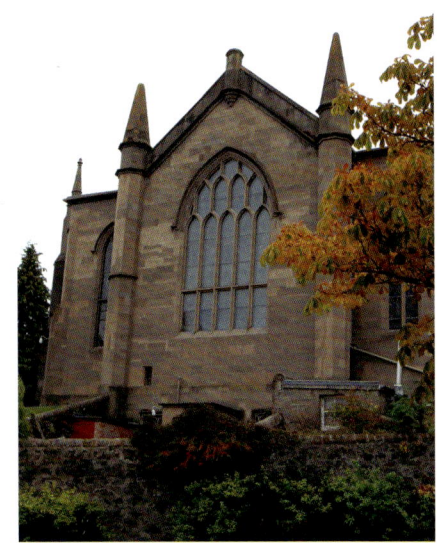

bridge. If you look up to your right you will see Kinnoull Church which has a wonderful stained glass window based on drawings by Millais **(53)**. Further along you will see the remains of a slipway and gate which are believed to date from the early-18th century. Adjacent to these used to be the Old Ferry House which was demolished in the 1960s.

Take the path through the flats and apartments at the end **(54)** – these were built in 1978 and won many awards, both local and national, and even featured

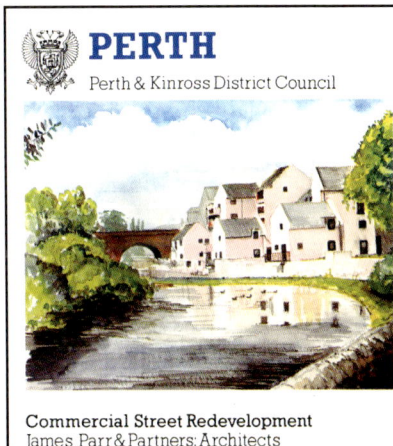

55 *Reproduced courtesy of A.K. Bell Local Studies Dept.*

56 © *PKHT*

on a postage stamp! Climb up the steps by the **Cross Keys Inn (55)** which dates from the end of the 18th century and was probably one of several establishments offering accommodation, refreshment and stabling for travellers.

Turn left and return to the centre of town via Smeaton's Bridge, or the Old Bridge as it is also known. On your left you will pass the **Toll House (56)** – a reminder of the days when people had to pay a toll to cross the bridge. The bridge, as mentioned earlier, was opened in 1771 and was used for livestock as well as people and vehicles. As early as 1813 there were complaints that the bridge was not wide enough and in 1869 the stone parapets were removed and footpaths added, supported on iron brackets.

Walking over the bridge you have more magnificent views, both downstream in the direction you have come from, and upstream to the North Inch and the hills beyond. As you reach the end of Smeaton's Bridge you will see, facing you, the **Marshall Monument (57)**, completed in 1824 as a symbol of gratitude to Lord Provost Thomas Hay Marshall. The building is in classical style with Ionic columns and a cupola and now houses Perth Museum and Art Gallery. The bow-fronted building next door to this was Perth's 'New Post Office' in the mid-19th century.